About the Author

Ramon Cott is a software developer, engineer, and entrepreneur with a rich background in technology, business, and finance. Over the years, he has built innovative solutions, from financial applications and medical systems to advanced web platforms for live video streaming. As the founder of Software Systems S.A., he developed accounting, invoicing, and payroll solutions, helping businesses streamline their operations.

With an educational background in industrial engineering and law, Ramon has also worked as a Chief Plant Engineer in textile manufacturing and as an analyst at the Dominican Republic Central Bank, evaluating industrial projects. His expertise in web technologies, networking, and cloud-based systems has allowed him to create scalable platforms that serve global audiences. Passionate about problem-solving and digital transformation, he continues to develop solutions that bridge industries with technology.

Igniting the Future: Humanity's Evolution from Fire to AI

Curiosity, Resilience, and Perseverance: Unlocking the Impossible

Ramon Cott
3/15/2025

Humanity's journey has been defined by curiosity and perseverance, driving transformations that reshape civilization. From the discovery of fire to the rise of language, agriculture, industry, and digital technology, each leap has expanded our potential.

Now, we approach the next great singularity, the fusion of human and artificial intelligence. While many have speculated on this interface, few have explored the true impact it will have on human intelligence. Unlike past technological advancements that required a learning curve, limiting users from fully harnessing their potential, this direct interface will remove that barrier entirely. Knowledge will no longer be something to acquire through effort and adaptation, it will be instantly accessible, seamlessly integrated into human cognition.

By reflecting on past milestones, this document serves as both a guide and an inspiration, illustrating that every breakthrough, past and future, begins with the courage to embrace the unknown. The coming singularity will not just enhance human intelligence; it will redefine what it means to learn, think, and innovate.

Table of Contents

01 - Prologue

Curiosity, Resilience, and Perseverance: Unlocking the Impossible

"The impossible can be done."

Franklin D. Roosevelt

T he story goes that when military planners expressed doubts about the feasibility of launching bombers from an aircraft carrier to strike Japan, Roosevelt responded with this phrase and, in a rare moment, stood up from his wheelchair to emphasize his determination.

Figure 1: Depiction of the Doolittle Raid; B-25 Mitchell bombers taking off from the USS Hornet, April 18, 1942. This historic mission marked the first U.S. air raid on Japan during World War II, showcasing American resilience and strategic ingenuity.

This statement embodies the spirit of perseverance and determination in the face of overwhelming odds. It reminds us that even when challenges seem insurmountable, with courage, ingenuity, and unwavering belief, success is possible.

1. Defy the Impossible: Great victories are born from the willingness to challenge limitations. History is shaped by those who refuse to accept "impossible" as an answer. When you're told something can't be done, see it as an opportunity to prove otherwise.

2. Take Bold Action: Roosevelt and his team didn't dwell on setbacks; they took immediate action. Likewise, instead of focusing on barriers, channel energy into solutions. Boldness attracts opportunity.

3. Lead with Vision: In difficult times, people look for leadership. Roosevelt's belief that "the impossible can be done" inspired an entire nation. Your determination can ignite confidence in others.

4. Adapt and Overcome: The Doolittle Raid wasn't perfect; it was a daring and risky operation. But it demonstrated resilience. Progress is rarely smooth; adjust, learn and keep moving forward.

5. Stand Up, Even When It's Hard: Roosevelt, despite his paralysis, found a way to lead with strength. His moment of rising to emphasize his words is symbolic: no matter our limitations, we can rise above them.

Throughout this book, you'll come across paragraphs written in italics and enclosed within single quotes. Think of them as signposts along this journey, guiding you forward. You'll find that sometimes, instead of giving a strict definition, we'll offer an example. Not to sidestep precision, but to make things clearer. A well-placed example can illuminate a concept better than any definition ever could.

'The next time you face a challenge that seems too great, remember: The impossible can be done. It has been done before, and it will be done again; perhaps by you. Keep pushing forward. '

02 - What is a Singularity

I s a term used in different fields to describe a point where the normal rules break down. Below are a few definitions, some with examples, as how they are understood in different disciplines:

- Mathematics & Physics: Is a point where numbers or physical properties become infinite or undefined. A simple example in math is dividing by zero; it doesn't give a meaningful answer. In physics, a gravitational singularity happens in black holes, where gravity becomes so strong that not even light can escape. Scientists believe that at the very center of a black hole, space and time as we understand them cease to behave normally.

- Technological Singularity: This refers to a future moment when artificial intelligence (AI) surpasses human intelligence, potentially changing civilization forever. Imagine computers and robots that can think, learn, and improve themselves far beyond human abilities. Some experts, like Ray Kurzweil, predict this could lead to rapid advancements in medicine, science, and even the way we live. However, it also raises concerns as to what happens if AI becomes too powerful for humans to control?

- Linguistics & Philosophy: In language and thought, a singularity can describe a unique event that changes everything. For example, human consciousness and the ability to think, reflect, and create this is often considered singular because no other species on Earth seems to have it at our level. Another example is the invention of the internet, which transformed how people connect and share information, marking a "singular" moment in history.

- Cosmological Singularity (The Big Bang): The universe itself may have started from a singularity! The Big Bang Theory suggests that everything began as an incredibly small, infinitely dense, and hot point before expanding into the universe we see today. Scientists don't fully understand what happened before this moment because the laws of physics break down at this point.

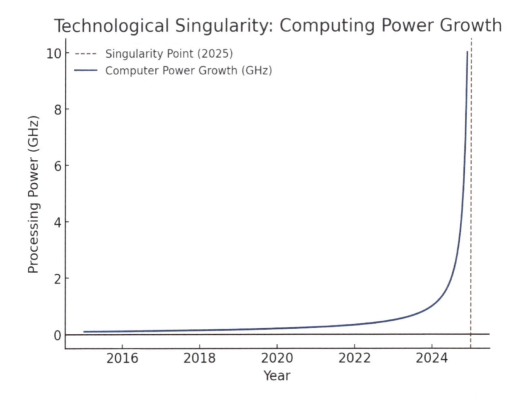

Figure 2: Graph illustrating the concept of technological singularity. As time approaches 2025, computing power grows exponentially, indicating a point where traditional predictions fail, symbolizing rapid and uncontrollable technological advancement.

Why Does Singularity Matter

Singularities are important because they mark the limits of what we know. Whether it's black holes, AI, or the birth of the universe, these ideas push science and philosophy to their edges.

Why is Used for the Unexplainable

When equations break down (like at the center of a black hole), we call it a singularity because we don't have the physics to explain what happens beyond that point. Instead of saying "we don't know", calling it a singularity makes it sound precise, though it still hides the mystery.

The idea of AI surpassing human intelligence is difficult to predict, so calling it "the Singularity" gives it an air of inevitability and sophistication. The term creates a sense of mystique, making it seem like a profound truth rather than just speculation.

The way singularity is discussed (especially in philosophy and AI research) often uses technical jargon that makes it harder for the average person to engage. It's similar to how ancient civilizations explained things as "acts of gods"; today, we use scientific or futuristic terms to maintain an aura of expertise.

Does the Term Help or Hinder Understanding

On one hand, it helps by giving a name to complex, boundary-pushing ideas. On the other, it hides ignorance behind sophistication, making it seem like an absolute truth rather than a problem we haven't solved.

The Power of Singularity

At its core represents the moments when everything changes, when the rules we know break down, and something entirely new emerges. Whether in mathematics, physics, technology, or philosophy, is a point of no return, a leap into the unknown that redefines the future. From the discovery of fire to the invention of the wheel, from Einstein's theories to the rise of artificial intelligence, history is shaped by singularities; moments of breakthrough that propel humanity forward. Just as early humans tamed fire and reshaped their destiny, we now stand on the edge of another singularity: one where AI, space exploration, and new scientific discoveries might redefine life as we know it.

Singularities are not just barriers; they are gateways. They challenge us to think beyond limits, to explore the unknown, and to dream of a future where the impossible becomes reality. The journey of humanity has always been about pushing past boundaries.

03 - Singularities in Human History

Gradual but Profound Changes

As a point of no return in human civilization and transformations that gradually, yet irreversibly, reshape human civilization these are some "singular" moments:

1. Agricultural Revolution (~10,000 BC): Humans shift from hunting-gathering to farming. Gradual at first, but it permanently alters society leading to cities, economies, and eventually, empires.

2. The Printing Press (15th Century): Gutenberg's invention democratized knowledge, fueling the Renaissance, the Reformation, and the Scientific Revolution. Literacy, education, and mass communication became new pillars of society.

3. Scientific Revolution (16th–18th Century): The shift to empirical reasoning, experimentation, and the scientific method fundamentally changed how humans understood the world. It paved the way for the Industrial Revolution.

4. Industrial Revolution (~1700s–1800s): The steam engine, mechanized production, and factories changed everything. People didn't wake up one day and say, "We are in the Industrial Revolution," but within a few generations, society was unrecognizable.

5. Electricity & Communication (~19th–20th Century): The introduction of electricity, telephones, and radio sped up globalization. Again, people didn't realize they were in the middle of a singularity.

6. Digital Revolution (1950s–Present): The internet, smart phones, and AI are currently shaping a new world. People today don't feel like they're in a historical transformation, but future generations will look back and see it as a singularity moment.

Figure 3: Singularities in Human History: From the Printing Press to the Digital Age

These are just a few examples. The key takeaway is that all these transformations share common characteristics:

1- The Emergence of Something New: A groundbreaking shift, often technological or conceptual, fundamentally alters how humans live and interact.

2- Gradual yet Unstoppable Adoption: At first, the change is subtle, absorbed into daily life without people fully realizing its impact.

3- A Point of No Return: Once society adapts, there is no realistic path back to the "old way" of life.

4- Resistance and Conflict: Not everyone welcomes change. Every singularity has sparked resistance, societal upheaval, and political confrontations, as many fear losing stability, traditions, or power structures.

5- Unintended Consequences: Every major transformation brings unexpected side effects. The Industrial Revolution improved production but also led to urban overcrowding and labor exploitation. The Digital Revolution connected the world but also created misinformation and surveillance issues.

6- Shifts in Power Dynamics: Redistribution of power, whether economic, political, or social. The Agricultural Revolution led to land ownership hierarchies, the Industrial Revolution created new economic classes, and the Digital Revolution has concentrated power in tech giants.

7- Acceleration of Change: Each new one arrives faster than the last. The gap between the Agricultural and Industrial Revolutions was millennia; between the Industrial and Digital Revolutions, just centuries. The next transformation may happen in mere decades.

8- Existential Challenges: The risks that threaten civilization itself. The Nuclear Age brought the possibility of global destruction, AI raises concerns about human obsolescence, and biotechnology could redefine life itself.

Conclusion

History is not a straight path but a series of profound transformations. From the Agricultural Revolution to the Digital Age, each shift introduced something radically new, gradually integrated into daily life until it became indispensable. These changes are irreversible; no civilization willingly returns to the past once it has crossed these thresholds.

Yet, singularities are not merely stories of progress. They bring disruption, resistance, and unintended consequences. Every transformation has sparked conflict, upended power structures, and forced humanity to confront new ethical and existential dilemmas. As change accelerates, the stakes grow higher.

The challenge is not just to recognize these singularities but to navigate them with wisdom. The future will not wait for us to be ready. It is shaped by those who embrace transformation, anticipate its risks, and guide its course.

'We may be architects of change or reluctant passengers but history moves forward, one singularity at a time.'

04 – The Dawn of Wonder: The Birth of Philosophy

'A time when humans had nothing but their senses, their minds, and an overwhelming curiosity about the world around them'

Figure 4: As the first light of dawn touches the earth, so too does the light of curiosity awaken the human mind.

Imagine a time before science, before experiments, before even writing existed. Why does the sun rise and set? What are the stars? Why do people grow old and die? These were some of the first questions ever asked, and they set humanity on a path of endless discovery.

This is where philosophy was born, not in a laboratory, but in the thoughts of people who dared to wonder. Unlike today, where we have tools like telescopes and microscopes, early humans had only observation and imagination. They looked at the sky, the rivers, the mountains, and tried to make sense of reality.

The First Thinkers: From Myths to Reason

At first, answers came in the form of stories; myths about gods, spirits, and magical forces that controlled nature. These stories helped explain the unknown, but over time, some people began to wonder: What if the world follows rules? What if there are patterns we can understand?

This was the spark of philosophy. In ancient civilizations, especially in places like Greece, India, China, and Mesopotamia, some thinkers started asking questions in a new way. Instead of relying only on myths, they searched for logical explanations.

- In Ancient Greece, Thales suggested that the world might be made of one fundamental substance, maybe water!
- In India, sages explored the nature of existence, asking whether reality was just an illusion.
- In China, Confucius and Laozi asked: How should we live? What makes a good life?

These early thinkers didn't always have the right answers, but they started something powerful: they taught humanity how to question everything.

Why This Matters Today

The first philosophers were not scientists, but they paved the way for science. They taught us that knowledge doesn't come from accepting what we are told; it comes from questioning, exploring, and thinking deeply.

The spirit of those first questions still lives in us today. Every time you wonder about the universe, about life, about the future, you are continuing the tradition that began thousands of years ago.

'Philosophy was the first great adventure of the human mind, and it reminds us that curiosity is what makes us truly human.'

05 - Scientific Method: From Philosophy to Science

'Philosophy seeks truth through beliefs, while science uncovers truth through evidence'

For centuries, human curiosity has driven the search for truth. What began as deep philosophical reflections on the nature of existence and knowledge gradually transformed into a structured approach to uncovering reality; the scientific method. This journey from abstract thought to empirical investigation is one of the greatest intellectual achievements in history. As you read on, you'll discover how philosophy laid the foundation for observation, experimentation, and reasoning, ultimately shaping the way we understand the world today.

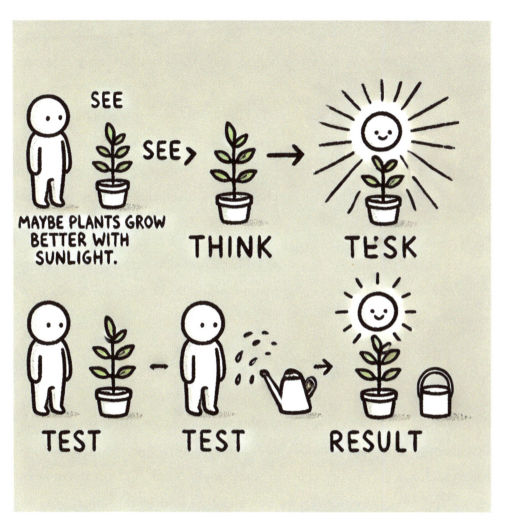

Figure 5: Explained in following paragraph

The image illustrates a simplified version of the scientific method using the idea that "Plants grow better with sunlight."

1.   Observation: A person notices two plants, one in the sun and one in the shade.
2.   Question: They wonder, "Do plants grow better with sunlight?"
3.   Experiment: They place one plant in sunlight and another in the dark, keeping all other conditions the same.
4.   Result: The plant in sunlight grows taller and healthier, supporting the idea.

This basic process reflects how humans naturally explore and understand the world through observation, questioning, experimentation, and learning from repeated results.

Birth of the Scientific Method

As we know it today, was born from the deep philosophical inquiries of early thinkers. For centuries, philosophy sought to explain the world through logic, reasoning, and observation. However, as human curiosity expanded, mere speculation was no longer enough; there was a need for structured inquiry, testing, and verifiable proof. This shift marked the birth of the scientific method, a revolutionary approach that transformed knowledge from belief-driven reasoning to fact-based discovery.

Ancient philosophers such as <u>Aristotle</u>, <u>Socrates</u> and <u>Plato</u> laid the groundwork for systematic thinking. They asked fundamental questions about nature, existence, and the cosmos, using rational thought to seek answers. However, their approach relied heavily on abstract reasoning rather than empirical proof. Aristotle, for instance, believed in observing nature, but his conclusions were often based on assumptions rather than experiments.

The First Tools of the Scientific Method

The real transformation began when thinkers started to challenge traditional philosophical ideas with empirical observations. The development of logic, mathematics, and systematic experimentation laid the foundation for what would become the scientific method. Key figures like <u>Alhazen (Ibn al-Haytham)</u> in the Islamic Golden Age introduced the concept of controlled experiments, emphasizing observation and hypothesis testing.

During the Renaissance, visionaries like <u>Galileo Galilei</u> and <u>Francis Bacon</u> formalized the principles of scientific inquiry. Bacon's inductive reasoning and Galileo's experimentation with motion and astronomy were crucial in shifting knowledge from speculative philosophy to testable science.

The Evolution of the Scientific Method

The scientific method continued to evolve through the Enlightenment, where thinkers like Isaac Newton combined observation, mathematics, and experimentation to develop universal laws of nature. As centuries passed, science refined its approach by introducing peer review, statistical analysis, and repeatable experiments, ensuring that discoveries were not just individual insights but universally accepted truths. Today, it remains the backbone of discovery, guiding research in every field from medicine to space exploration.

'What started as philosophical curiosity has become the most powerful tool for understanding reality, proving that while philosophy asks "why," science finds "how."'

Does Philosophy Have a Place in a Science-Driven World

It is far from doomed, even in the 21st century with the powerful tools of the scientific method at our disposal. In fact, it remains crucial for several reasons:

- Science Relies on Philosophical Foundations: The scientific method itself is built on principles like logic, empiricism, and the ability to test and disprove ideas. Questions like What counts as knowledge?, What is causality?, and How do we define reality? Are fundamentally philosophical.

- Ethics and Morality: Science can tell us how to build artificial intelligence, genetically modify humans, or manipulate ecosystems, but it cannot tell us whether we should do these things. Ethics, a branch of philosophy, helps guide responsible scientific progress.

- Interpretation of Science: Even with vast amounts of data, interpreting results and understanding their implications require philosophical reasoning. For example, debates in quantum mechanics or the philosophy of mind still hinge on unresolved philosophical issues.

- Limits of Science: Some questions remain outside the scope of empirical science, such as why is there something rather than nothing? or what is consciousness? Philosophy helps us grapple with these issues.

- Bridging Disciplines: Many modern fields, such as philosophy of science, philosophy of mathematics, and philosophy of mind, actively contribute to scientific discourse by clarifying concepts and methods.

Rather than being doomed, philosophy continues to evolve and work alongside science, refining our understanding of reality, ethics, and existence itself. It's not a competition; science and philosophy complement each other.

Understanding and Applying the Scientific Method

It is a structured, logical approach to discovering truths about the world; a process that moves from observation to questioning, hypothesis formation, experimentation, and conclusion. Unlike philosophical reasoning alone, which relies on beliefs and logic, it demands evidence and repeatability to confirm ideas.

The beauty of the scientific method is that it is not limited to scientists; it can be applied by anyone seeking to solve problems or understand the world more clearly.

Here's how you can use it in daily life:

1. Observe: Notice a pattern or problem in your environment. (e.g., "My phone battery drains faster when I use certain apps.")

2. Ask a Question: Formulate a clear question. ("Do social media apps consume more battery than messaging apps?")

3. Form a Hypothesis: Make an educated guess. ("If I use social media apps frequently, my battery will drain faster.")

4. Test with an Experiment: Gather data by monitoring battery usage with different apps.

5. Analyze and Conclude: Compare results to see if your hypothesis was correct.

6. Repeat and Refine: If needed, adjust the experiment for more accuracy.

By using this method, whether in scientific research, problem-solving, or daily decision making, we can move beyond assumptions and base our understanding on verifiable facts. The scientific method is not just a tool of scientists; it is a way of thinking that empowers us to seek truth, challenge misinformation, and make informed choices in an ever changing world.

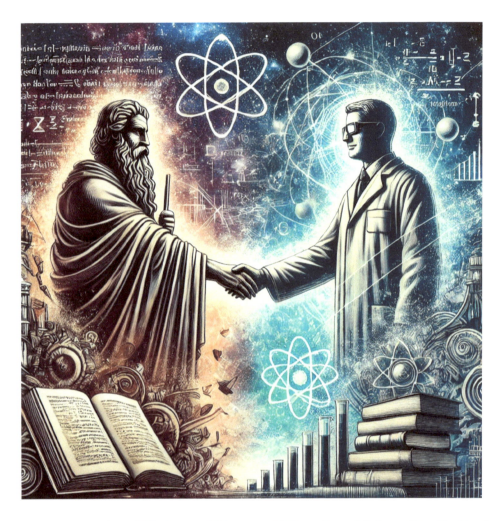

Figure 6: The Union of Wisdom and Discovery: Philosophy and Science Hand in Hand

06 - Comfort Zones: Forces behind Human Singularities

'Humanity stands at the threshold of its next great singularity; an extraordinary leap that promises to redefine the very fabric of our existence. To embark upon this transformative journey, we must equip ourselves with powerful tools: the deep, critical questioning offered by philosophy, and the clarity and precision inherent in the scientific method. Yet, as we strive forward, we face our greatest adversary: the comfort zone, a force tempting us toward complacency and intellectual stagnation. Breaking free from this barrier demands courage, curiosity, and relentless commitment. Now is the moment to venture boldly beyond comfort, driven by purpose and empowered by insight, as we shape the next profound chapter of human evolution.'

Figure 7: Breaking our Comfort Zone

What is the Comfort Zone

I t can be described as a psychological state where individuals feel familiar, secure, and in control. It represents an environment or set of behaviors and patterns that present minimal anxiety, risk, or uncertainty. While itself isn't inherently negative; it provides a baseline for well-being; staying too long within its boundaries can significantly limit growth, learning, and intelligence development. (Comfort_Zone)

The Traditional Learning Paradigm

In the 20th century, educational paradigms emphasized a fixed trajectory:

1. Early childhood education
2. High school
3. University
4. Work
5. Retirement.

Within this linear framework, society conditioned people to believe that formal education ends after school. Once entering professional life, individuals were presumed "fully equipped," capable of performing tasks repeatedly without additional significant learning or adaptation.

This created a comfortable status quo, reinforcing the idea that learning was complete. Consequently, it discouraged continuous intellectual growth and adaptability.

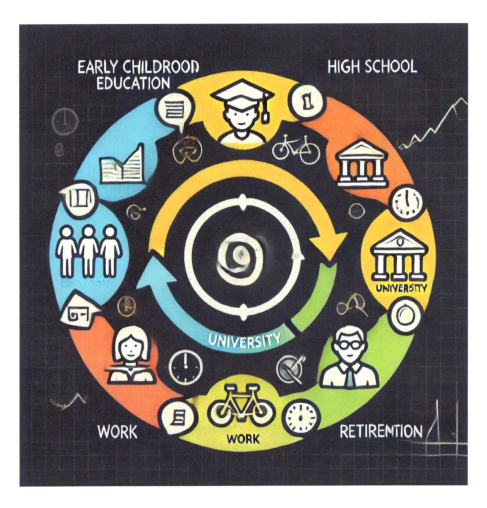

Figure 8: Life cycle progression illustrating the five stages

The Psychology of Comfort Zones

Defined by:

- Predictability

- Stability

- Familiarity

- Minimal stress or challenge

These elements, although psychologically reassuring, limit exposure to novel experiences and challenges critical for stimulating cognitive growth. Humans are wired to preserve energy, avoid stress, and stay within familiar boundaries, making it naturally appealing to remain in one's comfort zone. However, learning inherently demands exploration of uncertainty, risks, and unfamiliar environments; conditions typically found outside.

Learning Zone vs. Comfort Zone

The "learning zone" is an environment just beyond our comfort zone, where we encounter manageable challenges, uncertainty, and new information. It is precisely this exposure that fuels intellectual development and enhances problem-solving, creativity, and adaptability.

Defined by:

1. Moderate stress
2. Uncertainty driven curiosity
3. Questioning
4. Exploration
5. Knowledge acquisition.

Optimal intellectual growth occurs in the "learning zone," where individuals are pushed beyond comfort but not so far as to be paralyzed by anxiety. Extreme stress inhibits learning due to overwhelming anxiety. This zone is also not productive. (Yerkes-Dodson)

Impact on Intelligence and Awareness

When learning is limited by comfort zones, individuals become intellectually stagnant, reinforcing outdated knowledge, beliefs, and perspectives. This stagnation manifests as:

- Reduced Cognitive Flexibility: Difficulty adapting to new information or unexpected changes.

- Diminished Creativity: Limited exposure reduces the capacity for innovative thinking.

- Lack of Curiosity: Routine thinking suppresses natural curiosity, diminishing an individual's overall awareness and understanding of their surroundings.

Collectively, these outcomes translate into decreased overall intelligence; understood not merely as IQ, but as the ability to adapt, innovate, problem-solve, and understand complex situations.

Comfort Zone as a Barrier to Lifelong Learning

Today's rapidly evolving society and technological environment demand continuous learning. Unlike the predictable routines of the past century, contemporary life requires adaptation, rapid skill acquisition, and sustained intellectual growth.

Individuals who remain firmly within their comfort zone find themselves disadvantaged, unable to adapt effectively to shifting circumstances. They risk becoming obsolete, unable to grasp or integrate new knowledge, perspectives, or technologies essential for modern life.

Strategies for Breaking the Comfort Zone

To move beyond the limits imposed by comfort zones and encourage continuous learning:

- Embrace Discomfort Intentionally: Seek out experiences that stretch capabilities and understanding.
- Continuous Curiosity and Questioning: Encourage lifelong inquiry rather than passive acceptance of information.
- Incremental Exposure: Step gradually into new experiences, making it easier to adapt and expand the comfort zone sustainably.
- Growth Mindset Adoption: Believing in continuous improvement rather than fixed intellectual capacity motivates ongoing learning.

Conclusion

The comfort zone, while psychologically safe, imposes critical limits on learning, adaptation, and intellectual growth. The traditional 20th-century educational model reinforced the belief that learning ended after formal education, thus contributing to stagnation in intelligence and decreased situational awareness.

In contrast, continuous learning through deliberate movement beyond comfort zones promotes cognitive flexibility, curiosity, creativity, and intellectual growth, enhancing overall intelligence and awareness. The challenge of modern life is not merely to learn but to keep learning; to continually push into the learning zone, thereby expanding one's intellectual and adaptive capabilities.

07 - Slow But Unstoppable: How Resistance Shapes Progress

'Every chapter encountered until now has provided essential nourishment; ideas, insights, and tools carefully packed and stored, ready to sustain us. Like provisions thoughtfully prepared for an ambitious expedition, these earlier lessons and understandings serve as fuel for the long journey ahead, one that requires courage, vision, and resilience. We now stand at the threshold of the ultimate singularity: the merging of humanity and machine, a frontier that challenges our deepest instincts and pushes against our most basic fears. But remember this; while human minds are naturally reluctant, clinging to familiar shores, history shows we always find the courage to sail toward new horizons. Equipped with the wisdom gathered we are ready not merely to face this inevitable union but to embrace it, confident that resistance can slow, yet never halt, the relentless advance toward our extraordinary future.'

Figure 9: Breaking Free: Embracing Change and Unlocking the Wonders of Tomorrow.

The human mind resists change because it naturally prefers familiarity and comfort. Our brains are wired to seek safety and predictability, making us hesitant or fearful of new ideas, situations, or risks. Historically, this reluctance to change comes from our ancestors who survived by avoiding unfamiliar, potentially dangerous situations.

Throughout history, this tendency has often slowed progress:

- Scientific discoveries: When Galileo argued that the Earth revolves around the Sun, people rejected this idea because it challenged deeply held beliefs. His discoveries initially faced strong resistance, slowing acceptance and scientific progress.

- Social reforms: Changes like abolishing slavery or giving women the right to vote faced intense opposition because societies were used to old traditions and afraid of what new freedoms might bring.

- Technological innovation: New technologies, such as trains, cars, computers, or even the internet, initially frightened people who feared losing their jobs or facing unknown dangers, causing delays in widespread adoption.

However, even though our reluctance can slow down progress, history shows it cannot ultimately stop it. Eventually, the benefits and necessity of new ideas and innovations become undeniable. Once enough people recognize this, changes spread rapidly. Over time, curiosity, necessity, and evidence overcome fear and resistance, leading humanity forward.

'In short, human resistance to change can delay progress, but ultimately, progress happens anyway because human curiosity and practical needs always push us forward.'

Beyond Resistance: Imagining the Next Human - Machine Singularity

In a not distant future, resistance will likely continue slowing the arrival or adoption of new singularities (such as advanced artificial intelligence, biotechnology, or space exploration). However, history repeatedly shows that while reluctance may delay major changes, it ultimately can't stop them. Eventually, the practical benefits, competitive pressures, or the human drive to explore and innovate always overpower resistance. The next singularity; perhaps the profound merging of human consciousness with machine intelligence may initially frighten us, prompting debates, ethical dilemmas, and even outright rejection. Yet, as we've seen before, this resistance will gradually weaken, replaced by wonder and acceptance. Imagine a world where people seamlessly enhance their minds with artificial intelligence, overcoming cognitive limitations, unlocking previously unimaginable creativity, and solving challenges once deemed insurmountable. Although initially cautious and hesitant, humanity will step confidently into this remarkable future, as curiosity and necessity inevitably triumph over fear.

08 - Artificial Intelligence: Unlocking the Door to Infinite Possibilities

'Artificial Intelligence (AI) isn't just a fascinating technology; it's part of an incredible journey that is taking us closer to merging technology with human biology. In the not too distant future, AI will seamlessly integrate with our bodies, enhancing our abilities and fundamentally changing what it means to be human. This chapter explores how AI began, where it's heading, and the amazing potential awaiting us as biology and technology become one.'

AI is simply the idea of creating machines and computers that can think, learn, and make decisions similarly to how humans do. It's about teaching computers to do tasks that typically require human intelligence like recognizing faces, understanding speech, driving cars, or recommending your favorite movies.

Figure 10:

- Top-left: Man with Abacus

- Top-right: ENIAC Programming (1945)

- Bottom-left: 1980s Personal Computing

- Bottom-right: Autonomous Vehicle Driven by Supercomputer

A Quick Walk through AI's History

It didn't just pop up overnight; it has a rich, fascinating history full of big dreams, successes, and challenges:

Early Dreams (1950s - 1970s)

AI's journey began in the 1950s. The term "Artificial Intelligence" was first used by scientist [John McCarthy](#) at a conference in 1956. Back then, scientists dreamed big, imagining robots that could think just like humans. Early AI was mostly theoretical, but some exciting experiments began. For example, in 1956, researchers created the Logic Theorist, a program that could prove mathematical theorems automatically.

The Winter of AI (1970s - 1980s)

But soon enough, scientists realized AI was much harder than initially expected. Progress slowed down, funding decreased, and this period was famously called the "AI Winter." Basically, enthusiasm froze because results weren't coming fast enough.

Revival and Growth (1980s - 2000s)

It came back stronger when computers became more powerful and cheaper. Scientists developed new ways of teaching machines, like "machine learning," where computers learn from data, improving their skills as they go. This opened doors to real-world applications like detecting credit card fraud or recommending products online.

The Modern AI Boom (2000s - Today)

It exploded into mainstream awareness thanks to faster computers, cloud computing, and massive data sets. Today's AI can recognize your voice (think of voice assistants like Siri or Google Assistant), diagnose diseases (AI-powered medical scanners), and even drive cars by itself (autonomous vehicles like Tesla's Autopilot).

Understanding AI Today

Today's AI is typically built around something called "machine learning." Instead of explicitly telling the computer exactly how to perform tasks, scientists give AI large amounts of data, and it figures out patterns on its own.

For example, suppose you want your AI to recognize cats in pictures. Instead of teaching every single detail about a cat, you feed the computer thousands of images labeled "cat" and "no cat." The AI eventually learns patterns like recognizing pointy ears, whiskers, or fluffy tails and it starts identifying cats all by itself.

There's another exciting field called "deep learning," which uses something called neural networks; basically computer systems inspired by the human brain structure. These allow computers to handle very complex tasks such as translating languages in real-time, predicting the weather, or identifying medical conditions from X-ray images.

Where is AI Heading Next?

AI is advancing quickly, becoming smarter and more integrated into our daily lives. Here are a few exciting directions it's headed:

- Smart Homes and Cities: Your house could anticipate your needs, adjusting temperature, lights, or even restocking groceries automatically.

- Healthcare Revolution: Doctors might soon rely on AI to predict illnesses way before symptoms appear, improving prevention and treatments.

- Education and Learning: AI tutors could personalize learning experiences for every student, adapting to individual learning styles and speeds.

- Environmental Sustainability: AI could help predict and prevent environmental issues, like natural disasters, pollution, and wildlife extinction, creating a healthier planet.

- Creative Partnerships: AI tools may become creative collaborators, helping writers, musicians, and artists create amazing new forms of art and entertainment.

As it grows smarter and more capable, the possibilities are endless. But remember, AI isn't here to replace humans; instead, it's here to enhance our capabilities, making our lives easier, safer, and richer. We're at the beginning of an exciting chapter, and every one of us has a role to play in shaping this amazing technology.

Figure 11: Collaborative and optimistic relationship between humans and AI.

What is AGI (Artificial General Intelligence)?

AGI, or Artificial General Intelligence, is a future and more ambitious version of AI. AGI would have the ability to understand reason, learn, and solve problems just like a human across a wide variety of tasks. It wouldn't just specialize in one area; it could tackle virtually anything a human mind can.

In short, AGI would have the same flexible intelligence and adaptability that humans have.

What AGI could potentially do?

- Learn any new skill just like a human (e.g., cooking, painting, and playing musical instruments).
- Understand and have meaningful conversations about any topic.
- Adapt and solve unexpected problems in everyday life.

Summing it Up Simply:

AI (Narrow AI)	AGI (General AI)
Performs specific, limited tasks.	Can perform any intellectual task a human can.
Exists today and used widely	Still theoretical; does not yet exist.
Example: Siri, ChatGPT	Example: AI with human-like consciousness.

Where are we today

AI is deeply embedded in everyday life, powering virtual assistants, recommending online content, driving autonomous vehicles, and assisting in medical diagnosis. We currently have powerful Narrow AI systems that perform specific tasks exceptionally well, but we have not yet achieved AGI; the ambitious goal of developing AI systems that match the full range and flexibility of human intelligence.

We discussed AI's exciting potential, not as a replacement for humans, but as a tool to enhance human capabilities; making our lives safer, easier, and richer. Everyone has a role to play in shaping the future of this amazing technology.

09 - The Smartphone as a Mini AI Singularity

'Every time you pick up your Smartphone, you're holding more than just a device. In your palm rests an ever-evolving nexus of artificial intelligence; a miniature singularity that constantly learns, adapts, and anticipates your needs. From simple voice commands and smart notifications to personalized recommendations and autonomous problem-solving, they have become portable epicenters of daily life.'

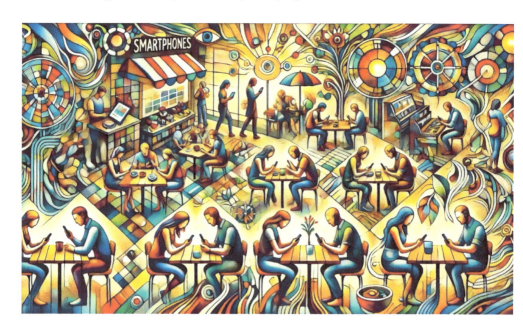

Figure 12: Human dependency on smart phones.

T he transformation of smart phones into what could be considered a mini singularity didn't happen overnight. It was the convergence of several technological advancements:

- Mobile Computing Power: The exponential growth in processing power has made them as powerful as desktop computers from just a decade ago.

- Cloud & Edge Computing: Offloading intensive AI computations to the cloud while integrating edge AI on devices allows real-time, intelligent decision-making.

- AI & Machine Learning Integration: Personal assistants (Siri, Google Assistant), predictive text, real-time voice translation, and image recognition have made them highly intelligent and adaptive.

- Hyper connectivity: Seamless cloud syncing enabled smart phones to function as hubs that connect and manage multiple AI-driven devices.

- Data & Personalization: Collecting and processing vast amounts of personal data to deliver an increasingly intuitive and predictive experience.

Miniaturization of Sensors: Face recognition, advanced cameras, biometrics, and augmented reality (AR) have transformed phones into sophisticated perception devices.

This convergence has led smart phones to become autonomous, learning-driven, and highly integrated with human life, closely mirroring the attributes of a Singularity in a micro-scale form.

Why are they a Mini AI Singularity

A technological singularity refers to a point where machine intelligence surpasses human intelligence, leading to exponential and irreversible changes. While smart phones haven't achieved full autonomy, they exhibit some key characteristics of a mini singularity:

Self-Learning & Adaptation: AI in smart phones continuously learns user behaviors and adapts, from recommending apps to predicting user actions.

Autonomous Decision-Making: From prioritizing notifications to optimizing battery use and suggesting routes, smart phones act on behalf of the user.

Real-Time Augmentation of Human Intelligence: Instant access to the internet, real-time translations, and AI-powered search make humans significantly more knowledgeable and efficient.

Interconnectivity of Intelligence: Smart phones are central nodes in AI ecosystems, linking wearable, home automation, and even vehicles.

Reduction of Cognitive Load: Smart phones handle complex decision-making processes that humans previously had to manually perform, such as financial management, health tracking, and social coordination.

While not an independent singularity, smart phones function as an extension of human cognition, seamlessly integrating with our daily existence in ways that are increasingly indistinguishable from autonomous intelligence.

Why smart phones Fall Short: the Learning Barrier Effect

Despite evolving into mini singularities, their potential is still hindered by a fundamental limitation: the complexity of their operating systems and interfaces. This paradoxically restricts their ability to truly democratize knowledge and optimize human potential.

- The Complexity of Operating Systems as a Barrier: They run on sophisticated operating systems (Android, iOS) designed for flexibility and scalability. However, this very complexity requires a learning curve, which goes against human nature. Humans are creatures of habit and comfort: If a user is accustomed to a specific way of interacting with technology, they are often resistant to change even if a better or more efficient way exists.

- Cognitive Load & Friction: Every new feature, setting, or update requires time and effort to understand, leading to frustration and avoidance.

- Digital Divide & Knowledge Gaps: Those who struggle to adapt to new UI paradigms, especially older generations or those with limited education, are left behind in the digital revolution.

- Fear of Experimentation: Many users hesitate to explore advanced settings, automation, or AI-driven features simply because they fear making mistakes or breaking something.

- Over-Reliance on Defaults: Instead of optimizing their experience, users stick to pre-installed apps, default settings, and limited workflows, reducing the full potential of AI-driven personalization.

This result in underutilization, meaning people are not extracting the maximum value from their devices, even though they have an incredibly powerful AI tool in their hands.

Overcoming the Operating System Bottleneck

While smart phones are mini singularities, they are imperfect because their intelligence is locked behind a user interface that requires learning. This slows down technological adoption, knowledge expansion, and productivity.

To unlock the full potential of AI-driven personal technology, the next step must be the eradication of interfaces as we know them, transitioning towards effortless, invisible, and deeply integrated AI assistance that requires zero adaptation.

10 - The Next Singularity: Intelligence without Effort

'The next singularity might not just be about AI merging with humans; it might be about how human nature itself changes when effort is no longer required. Will we still create? Will we still wonder? Or will we just consume AI provided knowledge without innovation? does this explosion of "smart people" actually make the world better, or does it create a generation that knows everything but understands nothing?'

Figure 13: Human - AI merge

What Happens When AI Eliminates the Need to Learn?

I f AI merges with the human mind, and interfaces become instantly intuitive, then:

- No Learning Curve: People instantly "know" things, no curiosity required.
- No Trial & Error: If AI guides every action, there's no failure, no perseverance.
- No Knowledge Gaps: If AI provides instant answers, traditional learning becomes obsolete.

This could lead to an explosion of "smart people", because intelligence would no longer be limited by effort or access to education. Everyone could instantly understand complex topics, languages, sciences, etc., just by interfacing with AI.

The Big Question: Is That Really Intelligence?

If curiosity, struggle, and perseverance disappear, does that means:

- People "know" more but think less?
- Creativity and innovation decline because challenges are eliminated?
- Society stagnates because there's no real desire to improve?

The human drive to learn has always come from necessity or deep curiosity. If AI removes those barriers, people might become "smart" in knowledge but hollow in creativity and critical thinking. Right now, the comfort zone is the biggest barrier to learning; most people don't push themselves unless they have to.

'Knowledge alone doesn't create curiosity, perseverance, or leadership; these qualities are inherent to human nature and are not automatically granted just because someone has access to vast intelligence.'

11 - The Next Singularity: A Higher Level of the Same Structure

I f the man-machine interface enhances intelligence and skill levels but does not inherently create leaders, innovators, or entrepreneurs, then the future may not be a completely transformed utopia. Instead, it could be a hyper-efficient version of what already exists:

- Massively Enhanced Productivity

- AI-enhanced humans would be able to work faster, learn instantly, and apply knowledge effortlessly. This doesn't mean everyone will create or lead; just that productivity will be at levels we can't even imagine today.

- A New Elite Class: The Builders & Innovators

Just as in every era of human history, a small fraction of people will emerge as the visionaries; those who see beyond knowledge and act on it. These people will create the enterprises, industries, and economic structures of the future.

AI won't remove the need for leadership; it will just give more advanced tools to those who already have the drive and vision to use them.

- Workers become hyper-efficient, but still workers

- Even if everyone becomes highly skilled, not everyone will have the ability to lead or create.

- Many will still follow and work within enterprises built by others; just at a higher level of efficiency and expertise.

- Leadership: The Irreplaceable Factor

- Leadership isn't just about intelligence; it's about vision, risk-taking, and the ability to inspire others. Even if everyone becomes equally intelligent, the world will still need leaders to organize, direct, and innovate.

This suggests that the future economy will still function in a hierarchy, just at a far more advanced level. This is not a new system, just an amplified one.

Conclusion

The AI-human merger won't create a world of equally ambitious people; it will just make existing structures operate at a much higher level of efficiency.

The hierarchy of innovators, leaders, and followers will remain but productivity and capability will skyrocket. Technology doesn't erase human nature; it enhances it, for better or worse. So the singularity doesn't replace capitalism, leadership, or innovation; it just takes them to an extreme level.

12 – The Next Singularity: A Fractured Society

'So far, we have explored what seems to be the next great singularity; the merging of humans with AI. However, as we have uncovered, this is not merely a singularity in itself, but rather a gateway to multiple cascading singularities, each reshaping civilization in profound ways. This fusion promises a revolutionary leap in intelligence, the eradication of traditional learning paradigms, and the evolution of economic and social structures into an ultra-efficient form of their current state. With every transformation comes disruption, and with disruption comes division. While some will embrace the limitless potential of AI-human integration, others will resist, fearing the loss of identity, autonomy, and the fundamental essence of human nature. This will lead to a fractured society; one half evolving into an AI-enhanced, hyper-intelligent elite, while the other clings to traditional human cognition, refusing to merge with the machine.'

Figure 14: Fractured Society as product of human AI merge.

History has shown that every major technological or social shift creates resistance, leading to division and even conflict. The next singularity; where human-AI integration transforms intelligence, work, and leadership will likely be no different. The challenge isn't just technological; it's about how society adapts to a reality where some embrace change, and others reject it.

The Singularity Divide: Two Faces of the Same Coin

Just as in past revolutions, society may split into two distinct groups:

- Adopters (The Enhanced Elite): People who fully embrace AI integration, enhancing their cognitive and physical capabilities. They gain access to higher intelligence, faster learning, and economic power. They will lead innovation, industry, and governance at an unimaginable pace.

- Resistors (The Traditionalists): Those who reject AI integration due to fear, ethics, religious beliefs, or personal choice. They may be left behind in terms of economic opportunity. Some may form independent communities, trying to maintain a human-only way of life.

This creates a new kind of segregation, not based on race or nationality, but on technological evolution.

Historical Parallel: The U.S. Civil War and the Fight over Progress

The Industrial Revolution created massive economic and social shifts, similar to the AI revolution. The U.S. Civil War (1861-1865) wasn't just about slavery; it was a battle between two economic and ideological systems:

- The industrial, mechanized North embracing change and mass production.
- The agricultural South, resisting modernization to maintain its traditional way of life.

In the end, technology-driven progress won, but at the cost of war and deep societal scars. This same pattern could play out in the AI Singularity era:

- One side embraces AI-human integration and thrives.
- The other side resists, fearing loss of identity, autonomy, and traditional values.

'The resulting conflict could be political, ideological, economic, or even violent.'

How to Handle This Imbalance?

To avoid an AI-fueled civil war or global conflict, we'd need strategies to bridge the gap between adopters and resistors:

- Ethical and Gradual Transition: People should have the choice to integrate with AI rather than being pressured into it.

- Education & Transparency: Just like past industrial transitions, clear public understanding of AI benefits and risks is crucial.

- Coexistence of AI-Enhanced and Non-Enhanced Societies: Different "zones" or societies might form, where enhanced and non-enhanced people can exist separately but equally. Example: Smart cities for AI-enhanced individuals, while other regions maintain a more traditional lifestyle.

- Economic Solutions for Non-Adopters: Universal Basic Income (UBI) or alternative economic models could prevent non-adopters from falling into poverty. A "parallel economy" could allow those who reject AI to still function and contribute without being left behind.

- Strong Ethical & Political Frameworks: Just as nuclear weapons required global treaties, AI and human enhancement will need strict governance to prevent abuse. The risk of AI elite controlling the world would need checks and balances to prevent a dystopian divide.

The Inevitable Tension: Can It Be Avoided?

Even with these solutions, history suggests that some level of conflict is inevitable.

The real question is how extreme it will be:

- Will it be a smooth transition with minor resistance?
- Or a major conflict, like the Industrial Revolution, Civil War, or Cold War, but on a much larger scale?

'Every major human advancement; agriculture, industry, the internet has divided societies between those who embrace change and those who fear it. The AI Singularity will be the biggest divide yet. If handled correctly, it doesn't have to be war; it can be a revolution that uplifts all of humanity, even if at different speeds.

The key question remains: Can we manage this transition peacefully, or will resistance push humanity into another massive conflict?'

13 - The Next Singularity: A New Socio-political Regime

Just as Marxism and communism emerged as reactions to the Industrial Revolution, the AI-human merger will likely give birth to new socio-political ideologies that attempt to adapt to the massive economic and societal changes. However, as history showed with capitalism prevailing over communism, the new system must be one that allows for growth, innovation, and stability.

Historical Parallel

Industrial Revolution → Marxism & Communism → Capitalism Wins

The Industrial Revolution created massive wealth but also worker exploitation, inequality, and social unrest. Marxism/Communism arose as a reaction to industrial capitalism, promoting wealth redistribution and worker control. Capitalism evolved, adapting to industrial progress through regulated markets, social welfare, and innovation allowing it to outlast communism in the long run.

Now, with AI-driven human enhancement, we face a similar shift: AI will create massive new wealth but also eliminate traditional jobs. A new ideological response will emerge, challenging old economic and political structures.

Possible Socio-Political Regimes

Here are some potential future systems that could replace or evolve from capitalism:

- **AI-Driven Hyper-Capitalism ("Cognitive Capitalism"):** AI-enhanced individuals will be hyper-productive, leading to massive economic growth. Corporations and entrepreneurs who best utilize AI-human interfaces will control the economy. Traditional jobs disappear, but the economy shifts to high-value AI-driven industries. **Potential problem:** If AI-enhanced individuals dominate wealth and production, inequality could skyrocket.

- **AI-Socialism ("Technocratic Socialism"):** AI ensures equal distribution of knowledge and resources. Universal Basic Income (UBI) becomes standard to compensate for job loss. AI optimizes governance eliminating inefficiency, corruption, and bureaucracy. **Potential problem:** Who controls AI? If a central authority manages AI, it could lead to authoritarianism or AI-driven dictatorship.

- **AI-Decentralized Societies ("Post-State Cyber-Anarchism"):** Power is distributed among individuals and decentralized AI networks. Governments weaken, replaced by autonomous, AI-managed communities. Cryptocurrencies and smart contracts govern economies without central banks or states.

  Potential problem: Without a central system, chaos or fragmentation could emerge.

- **Human-AI Meritocracy ("Singularitarian Elite Rule"):** The most AI-enhanced individuals form a ruling class, governing based on intelligence and productivity. Society is structured around "levels" of AI-human integration, creating a hierarchy based on cognitive enhancement.

  Potential problem: This could create a permanent underclass of non-enhanced individuals, leading to neo-feudalism.

- **Post-Work Civilization ("Post-Scarcity AI Society"):** AI automates everything, eliminating the need for human labor. No one works for survival, focusing instead on art, science, philosophy, or leisure. Society transitions to knowledge-based contribution, where people pursue creative or intellectual fulfillment.

  Potential problem: Humans might lose purpose, leading to cultural stagnation.

Which System Will Prevail?

History suggests that capitalism will evolve rather than be replaced. A likely outcome is a hybrid system:

- A mix of AI-driven capitalism (for innovation & competition) and AI-socialism (to prevent mass unemployment & inequality).

- Governments might adopt Universal Basic Income (UBI) while allowing free markets to function.

- AI governance could emerge to reduce inefficiencies, but humans will likely still demand some level of political control. Ultimately, the new system will be shaped by how AI is distributed.

- If AI is centralized, we may get a technocratic AI-socialist system.

- If AI is privatized, we may get hyper-capitalism with AI-enhanced elites.

- If AI is fully decentralized, we may enter a fragmented, self-governing world.

Conclusion

Who controls AI will not just determine the "political and economic systems" of the future; it will decide "the fate of humanity itself".

We stand at the edge of a new era, where intelligence is no longer limited by biology, and productivity is no longer defined by human effort. AI has the potential to "liberate us from scarcity", to "expand human capability beyond imagination", and to "reshape civilization at its core". But its power is a double-edged sword; wielded responsibly, it can "uplift humanity"; concentrated in the hands of a few, can "enslave us to a new hierarchy of control".

If AI remains "accessible to all", we could see the birth of "a decentralized world", where intelligence, opportunity, and progress are shared across all of humanity. A world where knowledge is no longer a privilege but a birthright, and where the barriers of education, economics, and power dissolve into something more just, more limitless, more human than ever before.

But if AI falls under the control of a select few governments, corporations, or the ultra-wealthy elite we risk creating a new digital aristocracy, where enhanced intelligence and economic dominance belong only to those who control the machines. The gap between the empowered and the powerless would grow wider than ever before, forging a world where the many exist to serve the few, even in an age of boundless potential.

The question isn't whether capitalism will survive; it is how capitalism will evolve to integrate AI, automation, and enhanced humans. Will it remain a system of competition and innovation, or will it become something unrecognizable? Will AI amplify economic opportunity, or will it create a system where only the enhanced can thrive?

The singularity is coming; not as a moment, but as a process, a transition, a great unraveling of the world we know and the emergence of something entirely new. Our choices today will decide whether this future is one of prosperity and shared intelligence or one of control, division, and unseen oppression.

'We are not just witnesses to this change. We are the architects of it. The future is not written. We must choose wisely.'

Bibliography

Artificial_General_Intelligence. (n.d.). *Wikipedia*. Retrieved from https://en.wikipedia.org/wiki/Artificial_general_intelligence

Artificial_Intelligence. (n.d.). *Wikipedia*. Retrieved from https://en.wikipedia.org/wiki/Artificial_intelligence

Comfort_Zone. (n.d.). *Wikipedia*. Retrieved from https://en.wikipedia.org/wiki/Comfort_zone

Deep_Learning. (n.d.). *Wikipedia*. Retrieved from https://en.wikipedia.org/wiki/Deep_learning

ENIAC. (n.d.). *Wikipedia*. Retrieved from https://en.wikipedia.org/wiki/ENIAC

Henry_Kissinger. (n.d.). Retrieved from thetimes.com: https://www.thetimes.com/world/us-world/article/henry-kissingers-ai-takeover-warning-from-beyond-the-grave-7mngdx39q?region=global

Machine_learning. (n.d.). *Wikipedia*. Retrieved from https://en.wikipedia.org/wiki/Machine_learning

Reid_Hoffman. (n.d.). Retrieved from vanityfair.com: https://www.vanityfair.com/news/story/reid-hoffman-ai-revolution

Yerkes-Dodson. (n.d.). *Wikipedia*. Retrieved from https://en.wikipedia.org/wiki/Yerkes%E2%80%93Dodson_law

www.ingramcontent.com/pod-product-compliance
Lightning Source LLC
LaVergne TN
LVHW072049060326
832903LV00053B/313